SANDWICKHILL

KT-161-952

Published in the UK in 1994 by
Schofield & Sims Limited, Huddersfield, England.

All rights reserved.
No part of this publication may be reproduced,
stored in a retrieval system, or transmitted in any form,
or by any means, electronic, mechanical, photocopying,
recording or otherwise, without the prior permission
of the copyright holders.

0 7217 5002 8

©1993 éditions MANGO

# Transport

Schofield & Sims Limited Huddersfield.

WESTERN ISLES
LIBRARIES
396/5923 J

388

# The History of Transport

The first steam-driven car.

The wheel.

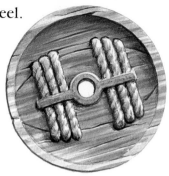

For a long time, people searched for ways of going further, higher, faster. They had the idea of using tree-trunks to make rafts to float on. Then they learned to use the wind and invented the sail.

The first steamboat.

The first steam locomotive.

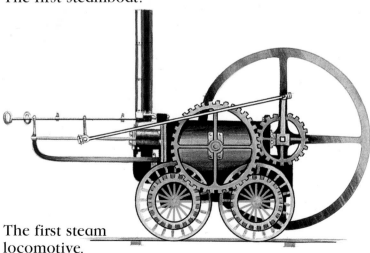

The first bicycle.

The first boats: the raft and the papyrus boat.

On land, people needed to transport heavy loads. They invented the wheel and the cart, which were pulled by oxen, horses or donkeys. Then the engine replaced animals, and trains, cars, steamships, aeroplanes and *rockets* were made.

The first aeroplane.

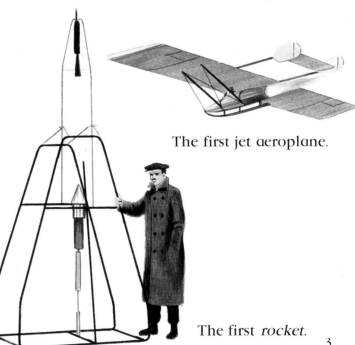

The first jet aeroplane.

The first petrol-driven car.

The first *rocket*.

# Sailing Ships

A long time ago, brave men ventured out on the seas to look for new lands. One of them was Christopher Columbus. One day, while he was sailing on the Atlantic Ocean, he saw land. He had found America!

The *Vikings* ruled the seas with their long ships that were powered by a sail and oars.

Galleons were big sailing ships that transported gold, *spices* and all the riches of the Orient.

Today, sailing has become mainly a hobby or a sport.

In certain countries, people still use boats called *junks* and *sampans*.

# Motor Boats

The big sailing ships of old depended too much on the wind, which was not reliable. But people still wanted to cross the oceans to look for trade. Steamships, then motor vessels, have made sailors 'masters of the oceans'.

*Container ships* transport goods from country to country. They can carry chemicals, wine, fruit and many other things.

In northern countries, the sea ca freeze in winter. The ice-breaker lets other ships enter ports.

The hovercraft, which transports passengers and vehicles, skims over the surface of both water and land on a cushion of air.

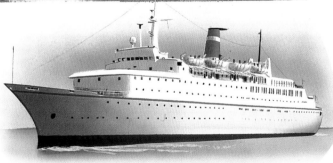

Cruise ships are like huge floating hotels with swimming-pools, shops and restaurants.

# The Seaport

Ports have always been places of refuge for boats and sailors. They are protected from wind and waves by their sea walls or breakwaters. Today, the big seaports, where ships come to load or unload their cargo, are vital for international trade.

# The Train

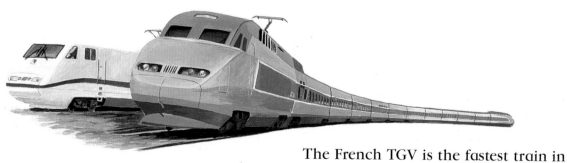

The French TGV is the fastest train in
the world; it holds the World Speed
Record – 515 kilometres an hour.

Long ago, the first trains ran on wooden rails. The carriages were pulled by horses which were then replaced by locomotives. Rails were later made out of iron. Trains can carry travellers and goods for long distances – from Paris to Peking; from New York to San Francisco.

Nothing stops the train. *Viaducts* were built to go over rivers and valleys, tunnels to go under mountains. Now, the Channel Tunnel links England to France under the sea.

11

# The Station

In the main railway stations, lots of trains arrive and depart all the time. It is vital to prevent them crashing into each other. Computers are used to make sure that all the trains travel on the right lines and arrive and depart from the right platform.

13

# City Transport

At one time, a bus pulled by horses was not able to carry more than a few passengers. Then underground railway systems were built in some cities. Now, throughout the world, millions of people use mass transport every day. They travel by bus, *tram*, train and the underground railway.

15

# Two Wheels

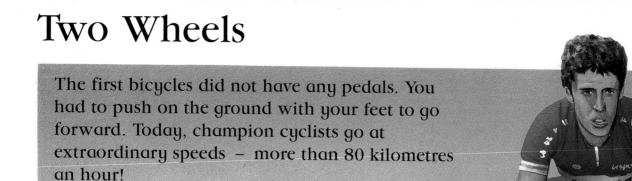

The first bicycles did not have any pedals. You had to push on the ground with your feet to go forward. Today, champion cyclists go at extraordinary speeds – more than 80 kilometres an hour!

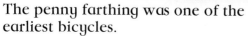
The penny farthing was one of the earliest bicycles.

In some countries, pedal-power is still the most important form of transport.

Motor cycles are used for transport
and for racing on special tracks.

Moto-cross is
a cross-country
sport for motor
cyclists.

# Four Wheels

Travelling on motorways or minor roads, crossing mountains or deserts, driving in the country – the car goes everywhere, day or night, in good or bad weather.

The Bugatti Royale was the biggest car ever made. It was nearly 7 metres long!

The cars used in motor racing have very powerful engines indeed.

To get a driving licence, you need to learn
the Highway Code. This gives advice to
road-users and helps to control traffic.

# Aeroplanes

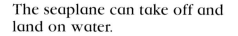

The seaplane can take off and land on water.

This Canadian aeroplane skims the surface of a lake to fill its special tanks with water to drop on forest fires.

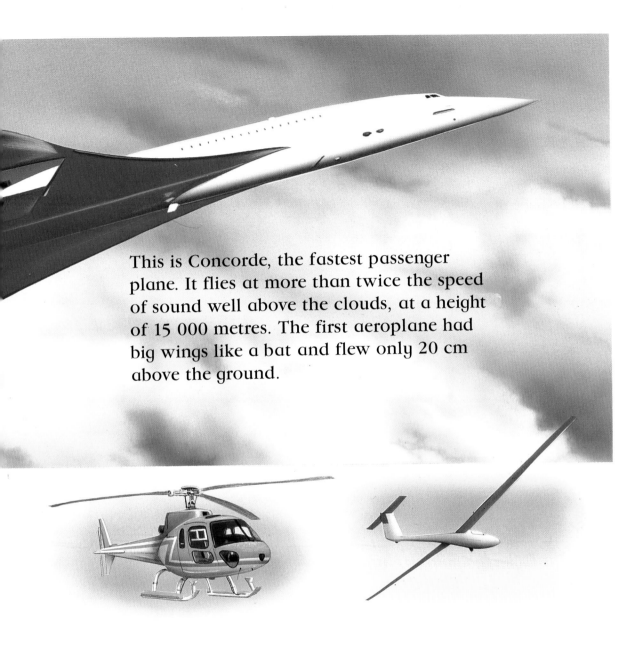

This is Concorde, the fastest passenger plane. It flies at more than twice the speed of sound well above the clouds, at a height of 15 000 metres. The first aeroplane had big wings like a bat and flew only 20 cm above the ground.

A helicopter can hover and can fly in all directions, even backwards.

A glider has no motor. It is so light that, like a kite, it glides on air currents.

# The Airport

At any one time, thousands of aeroplanes are
taking off and landing at all the world's airports.
In the control tower, air-traffic controllers track
on their radar screens the course of every aircraft.
They tell the pilots by radio at what height
they should fly and which runway is reserved
for them.

# The Space Shuttle

At the present time, the space shuttle is the only vehicle that can make more than one trip into space and back to Earth.

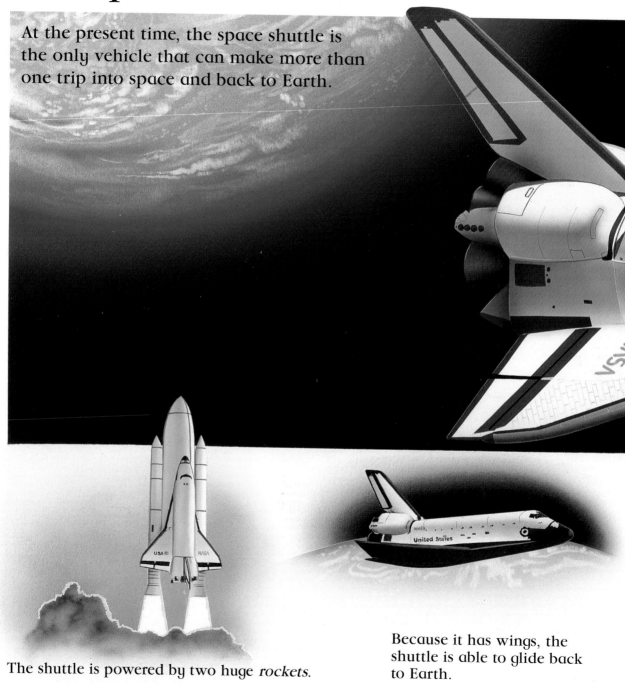

The shuttle is powered by two huge *rockets*.

Because it has wings, the shuttle is able to glide back to Earth.

The shuttle is tracked from Ground Control at all times.

It lands like an aeroplane on a very long runway.

# Glossary

**Container ship**
A ship designed to carry containers of goods.

**Junk**
A sailing boat commonly found in Asia.

**Rocket**
A very powerful motor capable of powering an object into space.

**Sampan**
A bamboo boat that is lived on in certain parts of Asia.

**Spices**
Pepper, cinnamon, vanilla and ginger are spices. They are used to flavour foods.

**Tram**
A means of land transport that is driven by electricity and travels on rails.

**Viaduct**
A bridge built across a valley to transport cars and trains.

**Viking**
The name means 'sea warrior'. Vikings came from Scandinavia in northern Europe.